TIMPSON
ON THE
VERGE 2

❧ ❧

D1424177

More village signs investigated by

John Timpson

Photographs by John Bacon
and Nicolette Hallett

Larks Press

Published by the Larks Press
Ordnance Farmhouse, Guist Bottom,
Dereham, Norfolk NR20 5PF
01328 829207
www.booksatlarkspress.co.uk

April 2002

Printed by the Lanceni Press,
Garrood Drive, Fakenham, Norfolk

British Library Cataloguing-in-Publication data
A catalogue record for this book is available from
the British Library

Photographs on the cover and on pages 6, 7, 8, 12, 16, 17, 23, 24, 25, 32, 35,
37 (left), 40, 43, 44, 53, 54, 60 (bottom) 61 (bottom), 63, 74,
76, are by Nicolette Hallett.
All others are by the late John Bacon.

ISBN 1 904006 04 3

NORFOLK'S ROADSIDE GALLERY – UPDATED

This second selection of village signs covers a period of considerable expansion and change in the 'roadside gallery'. Many of Harry Carter's familiar wooden signs of the 1960s and 1970s are now having to be replaced, either by exact replicas in metal or plastic, or by entirely new signs. The Millennium provided a great incentive for this updating, and other villages marked it by erecting their own signs for the first time. The process began in 2000, and one of the last to complete their project before the end of 2001 was Flordon, where a Millennium sign was dedicated on December 9th.

There have been more individual reasons for a celebratory sign, apart from the Millennium. Brockdish, for instance, erected a new one to mark the opening of a bypass around the village, and Cobholm, on the outskirts of Yarmouth, is one of the first communities in Norfolk to acquire a sign through renewal area funding.

I have tried to include as many of these new or replacement signs as possible, to keep the selection up-to-date and also to illustrate the changes in style which are taking place. Traditional wooden signs with colourful carved illustrations are still being produced, and long may they continue, but we also have a three-armed metal sign at Gayton, for instance, and a wooden pillar at Bramerton with illustrations on beaten metal around the top.

Whatever their design, all these signs give great pleasure to passing visitors as well as the locals. But they can be a little puzzling too, for anyone not well versed in local history. At Hilgay, for example, why should a cannon be aimed at the parish church? At Sloley, who is that nonchalant figure grasping a goblet and casually dangling one leg over the front of the sign? And at Brampton, why on earth are two dolphins amorously sharing a scallop?

All is explained in these pages - but not on the signs. Would it be an appropriate way of celebrating this Golden Jubilee year, I wonder, to provide the more baffling signs with explanatory plaques? Meanwhile my thanks to all those patient parish councillors and amenities committee chairmen who have assisted me, one might say, with my enquiries. And special congratulations to North Repps, winner of my newly-created MIPEI award for the village with the Most Information-Packed Explanatory Inscription! I could only fit a fraction of it into this book.

JOHN TIMPSON

ACLE

Why 'Folly Tree'? Was it perhaps the Folly-Age?

Acle's triangular green has seen several changes since Harry Carter's original wooden sign featuring the Folly Tree was erected in 1974 - not least to the sign itself. After years of wear and tear it was refurbished and preserved in the indoor bowls centre, and a glass fibre replica took its place. Then that was removed for several weeks in 2001, while a protective metal shroud was put round the base. It finally reappeared last November.

The silver birch planted nearby to mark the Silver Jubilee still looks a bit spindly after 25 years, but a plane tree planted a year or two later, just across the road, is already quite impressive. This is the one that replaced the Folly Tree shown on the sign, after it succumbed to Dutch elm disease.

Nobody is quite sure how it got its name. John Harris, who helped me with all this information, says a local history offers two theories. It may have been thought foolish to be so close to the road, though it was there long before today's heavy traffic. More probably it grew on the site of a former Folly, but no evidence of that remains. Maybe having a Folly Tree just seemed appropriate, in what might be called the Folly-Age.

The two-sided sign also features the old bridge over the Bure, a wherry, a waggon and horses, and St Edmund's church, with the crest of St Edmund below.

ATTLEBOROUGH

No cider-making now, but the turkeys and brushes survive

On both sides of the sign the pictures depict cider-making, an industry which was still going strong in Attleborough when the sign was erected in 1975. Unfortunately in recent years the William Gaymer Cider Company has closed down, and its nineteen acres of cider-apple orchards have been presented to the town and converted into a sports field.

The Gaymer family originally produced the cider at their family home, Banham Manor, a few miles outside the town. They opened the Attleborough factory in 1896, and at its peak it produced a refreshing 28 million gallons of cider a year. But the pictures on the sign go back much further, to the 17th-century *Vinetum Britannicum*, a sort of early Good Wine Guide. On one side an energetic chap is operating the apple grinder, and on the other a more elegant figure is grasping the lever of a screw press for extracting the juice from the pulp - though he shows no inclination to operate it. Perhaps the open barrel beside him accounts for his carefree attitude.

The besoms and turkeys under the pictures represent other local industries, which happily have survived to some degree – brush-making and turkey-rearing. The turkeys used to be walked to London for the Christmas markets.

AYLSHAM

A swashbuckling soldier, or a sober squire?

Harry Carter's original sign, given by the Women's Institute in 1972, had already been replaced - perhaps surprisingly - by 1983 with the same basic design but a rather different John of Gaunt. Even the spelling of his title was changed. In the earlier one he was a dashing figure in a jaunty plumed hat, mounted on a rearing horse, and the inscription described him informally as 'John O'Gaunt'. The present sign has a soberly-dressed rider on a more docile horse, and 'John of Gaunt' is spelt out in full.

I am not sure which is the more accurate portrayal, but judging by the history books I would go for the original spirited version. After all, John of Gaunt (or Ghent) spent half his adult life abroad, mostly on military ventures, and obviously enjoyed a good scrap. But perhaps Aylsham only saw his more serious side, after his father Edward III gave him the Manor of Aylsham and he held his Court in the Guildhall.

He took his responsibilities seriously enough, so it is said, to found St Michael's church, and there on the sign beneath him is St Michael, with shining armour and a sword. Above the sign is John of Gaunt's coat of arms, copied from the one on the original version which is now in the Council offices at the Town Hall.

BANHAM

Both sides may look the same, but the artist had some fun

The two former local industries illustrated here don't often feature alongside each other on a village sign. The man pressing the apples is doing a similar job to those on the sign at Attleborough because Gaymer's of Attleborough grew some of their cider apples at Banham. The kiln, however, is a reminder that bricks and tiles used to be made from Banham clay.

The two sides of Banham's sign look exactly the same at a casual glance, but they could well qualify for one of those magazine competitions to spot the differences in apparently identical pictures. On one side, the man with the press has an apple in his mouth, a cat is sitting on top of the pile of apples, and an owl is perched in the tree. On the other side, there is no apple, no cat and no owl. I gather there is also a mouse, but either it is skilfully hidden, or the years have worn it away, because I failed to spot it.

These little adjustments give an unexpected twist to an otherwise orthodox sign. Full marks to Mr Steve Egleton who devised it.

BEESTON (See back cover)

Not just a pretty spire – there's a world champion and flying Crusaders

Beeston's original wooden sign, celebrating the Silver Jubilee, mainly featured the arms of the former Lord of the Manor with a plough above it. The new one, erected to mark the Millennium, is rather more elaborate.

The main painting depicts a rural scene with grazing sheep, a ploughman, a pheasant, and in the background the fourteenth-century church of St Mary the Virgin with its distinctive spire. On the post below, is a drawing of Jem Mace, the local blacksmith's son who won the heavyweight championship of the world and became known as the father of modern scientific boxing. There is also the roundel of the American 392nd Bomb Group, 'The Crusaders', who were based locally during the last war. One of their Liberators is shown flying above the church, and the new sign was a major point of interest when survivors of the Bomb Group and their relatives revisited Beeston in 2001.

Appropriately the ironwork on the sign was made by Rodney Skipper, who looks after the American memorial in the village, and the painting is by his wife Susan. It was designed as a joint effort by the parish councillors and their wives.

4

BINHAM

A siege, a royal rescue, a demented ghost – it all happened here

Parish churches often appear on village signs, but not many of them look as dramatic as the Priory Church of St Mary at Binham. Wymondham Abbey is comparable, and it does indeed feature above the Wymondham sign (see the first *On the Verge*) but the whole of Binham's sign is devoted to a splendid painting of the half-ruined Priory. It was erected in 1994 at the instigation of the then Parish Council chairman, Mr George Bird, and the painting was by a local artist, Geoffrey Neale, who gave his services free.

The Priory's history was action-packed. It was put under siege in 1212 by Robert FitzWalter, who objected to the dismissal of his friend the Prior; King John then led his troops to the rescue with the cry, 'By God's feet, either I or FitzWalter must be King of England!'

Then there was Alexander de Langley, a Prior of Wymondham, who went mad through over-study and was kept in solitary confinement at Binham until his death; his ghost is said to haunt the ruins. And when Henry VIII dissolved the Priory, Sir Thomas Paston took over the site and sold off chunks of the stonework to builders' merchants.

Harry Carter, whose signs often illustrate historical events such as these, would have had a field day at Binham, but in this case the painting of the Priory deserves to have the sign to itself.

BIRCHAM

Royal connections - and an appropriately king-size ox

The three Birchams - Great, Newton and Tofts - lie on the edge of the Sandringham Estate, and parts were acquired by the Estate about sixty years ago. Since then there have been a number of links with the Royal Family, and the Royal Arms on the sign make this point. For instance, the new primary school was built on land presented by George VI, and the Queen Mother visited the school in 1998 to mark its fiftieth anniversary and rename it the King George VI School.

The central feature of the sign, however, recalls a much earlier era. Several Norfolk signs depict a ploughman and a team of horses, but at Bircham the plough is being drawn by a very substantial ox, symbolising the days when arable farming was originally introduced into the area. At first glance the ploughman appears to be wearing a crash-helmet, which seems a bit over-cautious even with so large a beast to control, but in fact it is the headgear of an early serf.

There is also a plaque recording that the sign was presented to the Queen in 1960 by the 1st Bircham Boy Scout and Girl Guide troops. The Queen happily is still with us, but the Bircham Scouts and Guides have long since disbanded.

BODHAM

The taxman cometh

Bodham means 'Boda's homestead' and Boda is portrayed on the sign as an apparently benevolent old gentleman seated under a tree, holding out his hand to a small child while assorted villagers and animals stand by. On the face of it a typical pastoral scene, with perhaps the Lord of the Manor or a genial soothsayer having a get-together with the locals. But Boda's hand is not extended in greeting, his palm is upwards, and the waiting queue seems distinctly subdued. Boda, according to the Domesday Book, was in fact a 'moneyer', or tax collector, and Bodham's sign is probably the only one in Norfolk featuring an early representative of the Inland Revenue.

A moneyer did not just accept money. If the hard cash was not available he collected the taxes in kind. Hence the goose, the pig and the lamb.

When the local W.I. donated the sign in 1977 to mark the Queen's silver jubilee they could have chosen a ploughman or a shepherd to represent the village's farming history. Instead, perhaps encouraged by the signmaker Harry Carter, who knew his Domesday Book, they plumped for a less obvious but just as familiar character in the farming world - their own local taxman.

BRAMERTON

The pillar with the paradoxical onion

This, I suppose, is very much a sign of the 21st century, a far cry from the traditional carved and colourful creations of Harry Carter's day. Indeed, as you drive past this chestnut pillar at the entrance to the village you may not recognise it as a village sign at all, unless you spot the name carved vertically on the side.

Certainly you will have to examine it more closely to spot the illustrations on the metal panels round the top. Three of the four sides show fairly standard features of a riverside village - the parish church of St Peter's, the village hall, and a yacht sailing along the River Yare. But the fourth is a little more obscure.

It looks like an onion plant, and the inscription 'Allium Paradoxunt' bears this out. Allium is a genus of plants with a strong onion-like smell. But the genus also includes chives, shallots and garlic, and the panel actually depicts an example of the wild garlic which can be found in some profusion in the area from Bramerton Woods down to the river. Wild garlic is presumably a paradoxical onion.

The sign was erected in May 2001 with funds raised locally by Bramerton Amenities Society. It was designed by the Society's current chairman, Mr Bill Glover.

BRAMPTON

A fishy romance? Only a Roman knows

The two perky dolphins amorously sharing a scallop go back to the days when every well-dressed centurion had a handle on his helmet. The sign is a much enlarged replica of a bronze carrying handle discovered on a Roman site at Brampton - or *Brantuna*, as it is remembered - on the other side of the sign. The original handle is now in the Castle Museum.

A blue area under the dolphins represents the Bure, which was navigable at Brampton for sizeable Roman ships, and one of these is carved on the post. Also on the post is carved a collection of pots; nearly 150 pottery kilns have been identified in the area. Then there are the crossed keys of St Peter, patron saint of the parish church, and a replica of a brass in the church, known locally as the Brampton Maid - though St Peter might mistake it for the Virgin Mary. The keys and the Maid could also represent Brampton's two former pubs, the Crossed Keys and the Maid's Head. Finally the two shields represent the Brampton family and the Marshams from the village of that name, who intermarried.

I learned all this from Tony Hilton, who organised the erection of the sign in 1991 to replace a dilapidated metal one nearby, depicting Oxnead Mill and St Peter's. The new design was carved by the late Dan Chambers of Wakefield, a retired prison officer.

BRESSINGHAM

The judge was 'manifoldly corrupt' - but he did pay for the church

When Harry Carter and Bressingham & Roydon W.I. got together in 1974 to design a village sign they had plenty of local characters and features to choose from. For instance they have one of the few village halls in Norfolk which is a Grade II listed building - it was originally the old Priory's threshing barn. There are also the Bloom family's collection of steam engines and prize-winning gardens. The local characters have ranged from Sir Roger Pilkington, who rebuilt most of the church in 1527, to Alan Bloom himself, who would cut a striking figure on any village sign.

Instead they dug further back into the village's history and selected a thirteenth-century judge who was so dishonest, even for those days, that even the King noticed, and he was fined 4000 marks for 'manifold corruption'. Sir Richard Boyland retreated to Boyland Hall, just outside Bressingham, and his claim to local fame is that he paid for the erection of the earlier parish church in about 1280. Presumably he managed to salvage a useful fortune, even after paying that fine.

He is shown in his judge's wig and robes - which perhaps he also salvaged - outside the church, looking entirely unsurprised at this belated tribute.

BROCKDISH

Hoorah for the bypass - but the old sign lives on

Villagers have various ways of celebrating a new bypass that takes away the heavy through-traffic, and Brockdish decided to do so in 1996 by erecting a new village sign. It was unveiled by the two oldest residents at that time, Edith Mutimer (who has since died) and Patsy Keeling, whose names are preserved on a plaque.

The four quarters of the sign illustrate various aspects of village life. There is the inevitable ploughman, a blacksmith, a chimneysweep's brush emerging from a chimney, and a man shooting game, a reminder that there is still a game dealer in the village.

The previous sign, designed by Mr John Chipperfield to celebrate the Queen's silver jubilee, had quite a different theme and shape. It had a crosspiece, which illustrated the seasons of the year - a spring songbird, a summer hare, an autumn pheasant and a snowy wintry scene. Norfolk's county crest was the centrepiece, and rippling lines represented the nearby River Waveney, marking the county boundary. Unfortunately it fell into disrepair, but Mr Chipperfield, who still has a pottery in the village, intends to restore it and install it in the more sheltered surroundings of the village hall - in time for the Queen's golden jubilee in 2002, 25 years on.

BUNWELL

Boseviles and bricks, Turnpike and turkeys – they're all here

Richard Costello, who lives in Bunwell, has packed a wealth of information and symbolism on to the sign. The common feature on both sides is the fifteenth-century parish church, but it is flanked by a different scroll of names on each side. On one there are the names of the four manors which used to comprise Bunwell: Haddeston, Boseviles, Persehall and Banyards. On the other are their modern equivalents, the five portions of the village: Bunwell Street and Bunwell Hill, Low Common, Turnpike and Bunwell Bottom.

The rest of one side is then devoted to the former brickmaking industry, showing the special fork and spade used in the process - and of course a brick. The plinth of the sign is actually made of these Bunwell bricks. The other side features the familiar farming emblems of sugar beet and corn sheaves, plus a Norfolk Black turkey, a reminder of the flocks which used to be assembled outside the old Queen's Head Inn across the road, for the long walk down to the London markets.

Finally a plaque notes that the sign was erected in 1992 in memory of Mr Ron Arnold, the chairman of the village sign committee in 1989-90, who died before he could see the result of their efforts.

CAISTOR
ST EDMUND

'Caistor was a city, when Norwich was none...'

I suppose it was inevitable that when the sign was erected in 1954 it featured the portico of a Roman temple. These days there is a lot more to Caistor St Edmund than just reminders of the Roman town of *Venta Icenorum*, but even the fine old parish church is over-shadowed - literally as well as figuratively - by the east wall of the old Roman town. It is perhaps understandable that one writer described the church as 'farouche', which I see in my dictionary means 'sullen'!

But for the average visitor it is the Roman connection that counts. Venta Icenorum was begun about 70 AD, just after the Iceni rebellion had been crushed. At first the Romans just used timber, but in due course they erected public buildings in stone, including public baths, a forum, a basilica or town hall, and a couple of temples.

They left it all behind in about 500 AD, but the grid layout of their town still shows up in aerial photographs, parts of the walls still exist, and it is said that bits of the buildings survive too - elsewhere. The second line of my opening couplet runs:

'...and Norwich was built of Caistor stone!'

13

CANTLEY

Three churches, two birds and a wherry - but the sugar beet is the star

Sugar beet, Norfolk's most widespread if least attractive root crop, comes into its own on Cantley's sign - which, appropriately, is maintained by British Sugar. An impressive beet is upended among others in the foreground, nearly dwarfing the cock pheasant which faces it, if not quite so colourful. Between them is a nesting grebe while a wherry sails past on the Yare, and the towers of the three churches of Cantley, Limpenhoe and Southwood are in the background - but it is the rampant root which catches the eye.

The reason for its prominence, of course, is the sugar beet processing factory at Cantley, the first of its kind when it was built by the Dutchman Van Rossum, who introduced sugar beet into the Norfolk farming scene in 1910. During the annual winter 'campaign' it processes seven thousand tonnes of beet a day.

There are some entertaining legends attached to this area, which might have earned a reference on the sign. A headless horseman, for instance, is said to ride at midnight past Callow Pit, where a treasure chest - according to another legend - was hooked out of the water, only for a hand to reach up and snatch it back again, leaving just the handle behind. But in Cantley, headless horsemen and elusive treasure chests cannot beat the beet.

CASTON (see front cover)

It follows the original recipe - with extra ingredients

There have been some changes and additions to the sign since it was erected in 1970 by the local Amenities Committee - 'a body of public-spirited men who encouraged us all to improve our own village,' says the original plaque, presumably worded by somebody else. But Harry Carter's basic design has remained unchanged, although it is now in metal instead of wood.

It shows a monk or nun welcoming two pilgrims to a gabled building, which was a refectory house in medieval times, and later became Church Farm, opposite the church. Pilgrims to Walsingham came here after visiting a small college of priests at Thompson, a few miles away.

On the green near the sign is the base of an ancient wayside cross, and a few yards away is the fourteenth-century Church of the Holy Cross. Neither featured on the original sign, but there are line drawings of them on the back of the new metal one, erected in 1999. There are also drawings of the Old School, the Red Lion Inn, and the windmill, now without its sails, which used to grind corn just outside the village on the Watton road.

Under the sign is the 'Best Kept Village' plaque which Caston won in 1988, and a more recent shield inscribed 'Caston in Steel' by Mark McSteen - who did indeed make the new sign.

CATFIELD

A wildcat or 'Catta'? Some say it's the latter

Not unexpectedly, Catfield's sign features a cat in a field, but I gather there are some who argue that the village had a rather less obvious origin. It might be connected with a Saxon farmer called Catta, just as Caston and Catton are thought to mean 'Catta's enclosure'. Or the farmer might have been nicknamed 'The Wildcat' because of his ferocious nature. But for lack of any proof to the contrary, I am happy to accept the simpler explanation in the *Popular Guide to Norfolk Place-names*- 'open land where wildcats are found'. The cat in the field looks fine to me - and as it's black, it could be a lucky choice.

The rest of the sign is straightforward enough. The church, the cottages, the sailing boat, the tractor and plough with attendant seagulls, are all familiar features of Broadland. The swallowtail butterfly is a reminder that they breed nearby. The plaque below the sign records its unveiling in 1998 by John Francis, the well-known Anglia News presenter. He had been covering a story connected with the village and agreed to do some 'uncovering' as well.

COBHOLM

Memories of more rural times on Cobholm Island

You may never have heard of Cobholm. It does not feature in the usual Norfolk gazetteers and guides, it is not in the Diocesan list of parishes, and even one of its current residents, born and bred only a few miles away, did not know it existed until her husband found a house there.

It takes a large-scale map to track it down, and even then it is only shown as 'Cobholm Island' - which indeed it was, many years ago. Now it adjoins the A12 trunk road on a kind of peninsula formed by Breydon Water and a bend in the river as it flows into Great Yarmouth.

Officially Cobholm is part of Yarmouth, but it was once a village with one of the largest windmills in Norfolk and a lively trade in salt-extraction. The windmill and the salt industry have long since gone, but a community spirit lives on among the streets of modern houses which have replaced them, and last summer Cobholm acquired its own village sign, one of the first to be paid for by renewal area funding.

The mill and the saltbags are featured on it, framed by an imposing horse-shoe, a reminder of the horse-drawn Yarmouth landaus which used to be based here. Breydon Water is in the background - and watch out for that oncoming seagull!

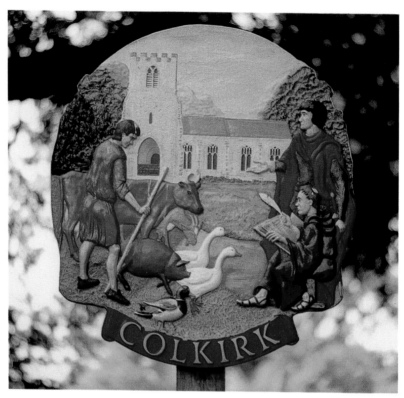

COLKIRK

A picture from the past, capsules for the future

The sign was erected as part of the village's centennial celebrations in 2000. It stands on the Camping Ground, which itself is an historic piece of land originally owned by the church and now acquired by the parish council.

On the sign a Norman scribe is making an entry for the Domesday Book, with the Lord of the Manor standing behind him. Colkirk takes its name from the Old English 'Cola's church', and the church is shown in the background, though whether this particular Lord of the Manor is Cola seems unlikely. The serf providing the details of his livestock for the scribe is certainly not identifiable from the entry in the book. I did make out a word that looked like Colkirk, but my Old English was not up to working out the rest.

Perhaps more intriguing for future generations will be the two capsules bricked up inside the base of the sign. One contains material from the children of the primary school, the other from local residents, illustrating village life at the turn of the century. If they included a can of Cola, it will bring the story of Colkirk full circle…

CORPUSTY & SAXTHORPE

'The Ploughman pay for all - and feed all'

The beam-type plough which was selected to represent the two villages also represents the two industries which used to provide their main employment. It is not only a symbol of agriculture but a reminder of the Saxthorpe Foundry, where it was made over a century ago. It was unveiled in 1974 by two members of the family who used to own the foundry, which was opened in 1800 by an engineer called Thomas Hase. At its peak it employed twenty men before it eventually closed in 1962.

There was another smaller factory in Corpusty which produced mineral water, but a bottle of water, no matter how sparkling, might not have looked quite as impressive as this plough to symbolise the villages. Indeed, the plough might have provided the idea for one which was erected in Stibbard two or three years later (see the first *On the Verge*), but in that case it was made entirely of farmyard scrap.

The Saxthorpe & Corpusty plough, as well as being the genuine article, has some little extras. In the base are canisters containing memorabilia of the 1970s collected by the local primary school, and on one end of the base is 'The Ploughman's Plea':

'The King he governs all
The Parson pray for all
The Lawyer plead for all
The Ploughman pay for all
And feed all...'

CRINGLEFORD

Rebels, royalty and rush hours - but things are quieter now

When the old A.11 trunk road from London to Norwich passed through Cringleford, thousands of motorists in countless rush hours knew this bridge over the Yare all too well. Then the bypass was built in 1974 and comparative peace returned.

The core of the bridge dates back to the early sixteenth century, when it was built to replace an earlier timber one, swept away by a flood in 1519. Since then it must have seen some dramatic moments. Robert Kett and his followers would have marched over it on their ill-fated rebellion. Queen Elizabeth and her entourage rode over it after she had said farewell to Norwich at the end of her visit in 1578. And in 1911 two farmworkers fell off it and drowned when their threshing machine toppled into the river.

The scene depicted on the sign is rather less spectacular. There is indeed a lady on horseback, but she has just a modest escort on foot. The fields and trees in the background still survive in spite of Cringleford's proximity to the city. But Harry Carter's original oak sign has been replaced by a copy.

One of the shields below the sign has a lion rampant from the arms of William de Cringleford, a thirteenth-century Lord of the Manor. The other bears the rather more recent emblem of Cringleford afternoon W.I., who erected the original sign in 1970.

DITCHINGHAM WITH PIRNOUGH

Spot the famous writer and a vanished village

The triangular shape of the sign is not just accidental, nor even an imitation of more standard road signs, and the pear does not just represent a local crop. They each have a particular significance, though hardly as obvious as the two ears of corn, symbolising farming and malting.

The triangle is intended to represent the Pyramids and ancient Egypt, a subject which fascinated Ditchingham's most famous resident, Sir Henry Rider Haggard. The author of *Cleopatra* and *She* was actually born in Bradenham, where the village sign features his portrait, but for nearly 45 years he lived at Ditchingham House, and the estate was the subject of his *Farmer's Diary* in 1898.

A clue to what the pear symbolises is the second name on the sign: Ditchingham with Pirnough. You are unlikely to find Pirnough on many maps or in many reference books these days, and its spelling has varied considerably, from Pirnough and Pirinhoe to Pirnhow - though it never quite became Pernod. It has been a 'vanished village' for centuries, though there are still the ruins of its church. Apparently the Romans used to grow fruit there, and Pirnough is assumed to mean 'pear tree on a hill'; hence that juicy pear.

DOCKING

A Saxon settler or just another water-lily

This must be one of the earliest decorative signs in Norfolk, dating back to the Coronation of George VI in 1937 - and it is also one of the best preserved, thanks to the quality of the natural oak on which it is carved. The intricate design does not stand out as clearly as a painted sign, but it is well worth a closer look.

It shows a man with his hand on a boy's shoulder, and in the background is a tree with a bishop's mitre in its branches. It would take an ingenious storyteller to link these clues into a legend, but somebody has done it. According to the legend, Docking is named after a Saxon called Docca, who in 1038 - and the date is apparently quite specific - was granted land here by the Bishop of Elmham. The sign shows Docca and his son surveying their domain, while above them in the branches the Bishop has thoughtfully left a reminder of who gave it to them.

I hesitate to spoil a good story, but according to a guide to Norfolk place-names Docking derives from the Old English word *docce*, meaning a dock or water-lily, and this was where they grew.

Never mind, perhaps both versions are true. And anyway, it's a jolly nice sign.

DRAYTON

The Drayton dray might be laden with extra meaning

As I found at Docking (on the previous page) there is sometimes an ambiguity about the origins of Norfolk place-names, which gives village sign designers a useful choice of subject. The 'dray' in Drayton could come from an Old English word meaning a dray or a dragnet, but there is also an Old Norse word meaning a load of timber dragged along the ground by horses. This sign looks like a mixture of these meanings, a horse-drawn dray laden with logs.

It would seem to ignore the 'ton' in Drayton, which meant a settlement or enclosure but is often illustrated by a tun, or barrel. In this case there is the ingenious theory that the dray's load of logs weighs exactly a ton, providing an alternative pictorial pun for the ton.

Whatever the reasoning behind the Drayton dray, it makes such an attractive sign that it might have merited a more central site on the village green. Instead it stands on a grass verge beside some traffic lights, and backs on to a pub. It marked the fiftieth anniversary of Drayton afternoon W.I., which unfortunately succumbed a few years ago. However, an evening W.I. was formed in 1970 and still flourishes; perhaps there will be a matching sign - in a better position? - in 2020.

EARSHAM

The mills have ground to a halt, but the otters survive

The most striking feature of the sign - and one I have yet to find on any other - is the carved otter crouched on top of it, still boasting its lifelike whiskers. It is of course a reminder of the Otter Trust established by Philip Wayre on the outskirts of the village, where its valuable conservation work has become a major tourist attraction.

The old watermill on the sign bears the name of Thomas Clarke and the date 1793. The artist, Mr Clarence Reeve, has inscribed a note on the back of the sign confirming that records show this is an accurate impression of how Earsham Mill looked at that time. He also notes that the Domesday Book recorded a mill on the same site, and in fact its successors continued to operate until the 1980s.

His picture shows a waggon laden with corn arriving at the mill, and behind it is the shingled spire of Earsham's fourteenth-century church. In the foreground are two herons, and there is a further selection of local flora and fauna carved on the post. They range from poppies and marguerites to a rather lonely-looking frog. Perhaps he is a bit envious of that lofty otter.

EAST BILNEY

He went to the stake - and his accuser went broke

1531
𝕿𝖍𝖔𝖒𝖆𝖘-𝕸𝖆𝖗𝖙𝖞𝖗 of
EAST BILNEY
1894-1994

When the parish council celebrated its own centenary in 1994 by erecting a village sign, there was an obvious choice for its subject - the sixteenth-century martyr Thomas Bilney. 'Martyr's Cottage', where he is said to have been brought up, still stands in East Bilney, and he features in a stained glass window, preaching from the Bible and then being burnt at the stake outside Norwich Cathedral. The sign combines the two themes and has him lashed to the stake, but with his hand upraised, still preaching.

One historian commented that Thomas Bilney's martyrdom 'seemed peculiar, even to the people of his own day, who were accustomed to killing as the penalty of a difference in belief'. He was ordained in 1519 and accepted much of the church's doctrine, but baulked at the worship of holy relics and similar teachings. Wolsey had him put in the Tower to rethink his views, and after a year he recanted. But a couple of years after that, he could remain silent no longer, and resumed his 'heretical' preaching.

When he came to Norwich, Bishop Nix had him arrested and put to the stake. It was perhaps poetic justice - or some other kind - that the Bishop himself was later arrested for exceeding his authority, and all his property was confiscated, reducing him (I like to think) to Nix.

EAST HARLING

...but it represents West Harling too

It is easy to assume that this is entirely East Harling's sign, as it stands in the centre of the village, but 'East' only appears on one end of it, below the lamb. The other end has 'West', and it does represent both villages, although there is little left of West Harling except the church, the odd farm, and the Dower House, formerly the Rectory, which is now the hub of a caravan and camping site.

This is one of the few village signs to survive virtually unaltered for nearly half a century, perhaps because of its basic simplicity. The life-size lamb recalls the lamb fairs, which used to be held each July in what was then a town rather than a village.

In the diamond-shaped panels on the post are carved the familiar emblems of a farming community: an ear of corn, a sugar beet, an acorn, a billhook, a rabbit. As the years have passed, an extra post has been erected in front of it to accommodate the plaques won by East Harling in Norfolk's Best-kept Village competition. It won the 'over 500 population' class in 1970, 1985 and 1986.

The sign was presented by the local Boy Scout group in 1953 to mark the Queen's Coronation.

EAST RUDHAM

Was the Virgin Mary seen in Rudham? Only passing through

This sign, like many others, incorporates the traditional emblems of a farming community - the ploughman, the sheaves of corn, the woodland, and of course the parish church. But it also features the seated figure of the Virgin Mary and her Child, apparently floating on a cloud. However East Rudham is not claiming to have shared the experience of Little Walsingham, made famous by a vision of the Virgin Mary. A little artistic licence has been used to blow her, as it were, off course.

The village was on one of the main pilgrimage routes to the shrine at Little Walsingham, and beneath the vision there is a procession of pilgrims crossing a high arched bridge - which if it ever existed has long since been flattened by the Norfolk Highways Department. As the cloud floats ahead of them, the effect is a little reminiscent of those Nativity scenes with the three Wise Men following the star to Bethlehem - and it is just as charming.

The sign was erected by Mr H. Shephard in memory of his wife, at the time of the Queen's Silver Jubilee. The imaginative designer was a Polish emigré, Mr Stanley Zdziebczok, whose name, I confess, I found rather more difficult to master than the meaning of his visionary sign.

EAST TUDDENHAM

An historic oak, or just another tree

The sign is in the shape of a tree, with plenty of metal acorns growing among the metal leaves, and a post that looks very like the trunk of a metal tree. Having learned from other signs that even the most obvious-looking features can sometimes have a very obscure reason for being there, I rather suspected that East Tuddenham might have had one of those oak trees which harboured the fugitive King Charles, or perhaps another of the 'Kett's Oaks' under which Robert Kett rallied his rebel followers. It was quite refreshing to be told that when the sign was erected in the late 1980s it was made that shape just to fit in with other trees on the green.

Framed by the branches are four reminders of village life over the years. The standing figure is Sir Edmund de Berry, a fifteenth-century knight whose family were Lords of the Manor for generations. Beside him is the parish church of All Saints, where there is an effigy believed to be Sir Edmund, holding his heart in his hands.

Also shown is the village pump in its little shelter, which still stands on the green although it has long since ceased to function, and finally there is the modern village hall, bringing the sign up to the present day.

EATON

The tun is for 'ton' - but is 'Ea' for elephant?

The 'Ea' in Eaton is an Old English word for a river, and 'ton' comes from 'tun', which meant enclosure or settlement, so it would have been logical - if a little unimaginative - to portray a settle-ment by a river on Eaton's village sign. But Norfolk likes to 'du diff'rent', and on many village signs the 'tun' is represented literally by a barrel or tun. There are examples at Old Catton and Watton; this one at Eaton is another.

The river is represented by the willow leaves on the spandrel, and the arms of the City of Norwich are a reminder that Eaton is now within the city boundary. But what about the elephant?

The sign was carved by Harry Carter, who liked to illustrate unusual aspects of local history, so did he perhaps discover that Eaton had a famous elephant-hunter, or even a circus proprietor, who might appreciate this recognition - and might even pay for the sign?

It was actually presented in 1956 by Mr F. R. Eaton of Eaton Hall, 0who neither shot elephants nor ran a circus, so far as I know. It seems Harry Carter merely felt that only an elephant was strong enough to carry a 'ton' - and everyone seemed to like the idea. In fact, when the elephant needed repair some years ago, enough money was raised to restore it, and they even turned it round to give passers-by a better view.

An heroic soldier, a famous authoress - and a mammoth conjecture

The parish church, a stretch of water representing two streams which rise here, and some trees to represent Felthorpe Woods are fairly easy to identify, but you need a knowledge of local history - plus a little poetic licence - to explain the Victoria Cross, the two ladies in a horse-drawn trap, and not least, the mammoth. Dr David Sladden kindly enlightened me.

The colour of the horse is a clue to the ladies' identity. Mrs Sewell and her daughter Anna lived for some years at Church Farm, where Anna first became interested in horses - and I leave it to you to work out the name of the black horse. The medal was won in the Crimea by Colonel Claude Bourchier, who died in 1877 and has a memorial window in the church. But the mammoth takes a little more imagination.

A pair of mammoth tusks were found in a gravel pit at nearby Sparham, and the bones of a mammoth were found at West Runton (their 'mammoth' sign is in the first *On the Verge*). Could they be connected? And if so, was Felthorpe on their route? Even if it wasn't, is it near enough to Sparham to be a mastodonic meeting-place? Well, why not...

The sign was given in 1998 by Mr Geoffrey Watling when a previous one of a different design, presented by his late wife, needed replacing.

FILBY

Norfolk's most shielded village sign

There are six heraldic shields, four of them representing prominent local families of the past, a fifth denoting All Saints' church, and the sixth bearing the emblem of the martyred King Edmund of East Anglia. Members of the far-flung Filby clan who gather here regularly may like to have a competition at their next meeting to identify which is which. If you are a Filby therefore, please don't read on.

On the far left are the arms of the Lucas family, former Lords of the Manor. Next are the de Warrennes and the de Valances, who were both granted land here by the Conqueror, and the cross on the end represents All Saints. On the post, above King Edmund's emblem, is a coat of arms which Filby competitors should certainly recognise - the arms of their own Ralph de Filby, a thirteenth-century Lord of the Manor.

Sir Ralph himself is represented by the figure on the left. He is confronting File the Dane, who got here ahead of all the other Filbys and gave his name to the village – 'File's settlement' in Norse.

Harry Carter carved the sign in 1975, but for once he did not design it. The heraldic shield enthusiast was a local resident, Peter Chapman. It is well shielded in another sense too - by attractive flower baskets and flowerbeds.

FINCHAM

The de Fynchams stand guard at Fincham Hall

Fincham has a number of impressive old buildings, but Harry Carter concentrated on the oldest and the most impressive of them all, Fincham Hall, for this sign erected in 1973 by the local Women's Institute. The W.I. emblem shares pride of place with the coat of arms of the de Fynchams, one of whom stands guard outside the family home, while his Lady watches admiringly.

The first de Fyncham, Nigellus, lived there in the reign of William II, and his descendants rebuilt it in the early sixteenth century. However, between 1572 and 1620 the Hall had four different owners, ending with the Hare family of Stow Bardolph, and various alterations and additions were made during the period. The north-east tower is the oldest to survive.

On the post beneath the sign is an orchid, representing the famous botanical gardens of Mr Maurice Mason. His collection of orchids and other rare plants came into the care of his son Hugh at Fincham Manor.

FLORDON

Could this be the last sign of 2001?

This little village of some 250 people may well have achieved the distinction of erecting the final village sign of 2001. It was put up at the end of November and dedicated on December 9th.

This was a village project organised by Flordon Community Group, financed by local contributions and created by a local designer and local craftsmen. The two main panels, carved on red maple wood, represent the ancient and the comparatively modern in the village's history. St Michael's church only has a Victorian bellcote instead of a tower, but parts of it date back to Saxon times and there are indications of where a round tower used to stand. The other panel is copied from an old photograph, taken when trains used to be a familiar sight at Flordon station.

In between are examples of the orchids that flower on Flordon Common, and one might think that these provided the 'Flor' or floral element in the name of the village. I gather however that 'Flor' is more probably linked with 'floor' and means a tessellated pavement on a 'dun', or hill. For the purposes of a decorative village sign, though, I rather prefer the orchids.

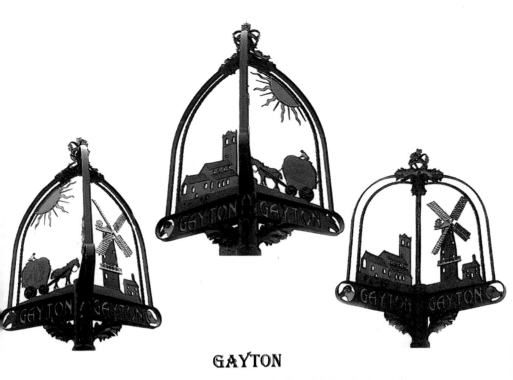

GAYTON

A hi-tech company in a low-tech (but high-rise) setting

Gayton's 1820s windmill is not only one of the main features on this unusual three-armed sign, it also helped to pay for it. The mill lost its sails in the 1920s and eventually became derelict, but System Three Technology Ltd moved onto the site in 1985 and its offices and boardroom are in the old brick tower - a modern hi-tech company based in a venerable high-rise setting.

It means that the old mill is again a main centre of business activity in the village, programming computers instead of grinding corn and baking bread, and when the parish council decided to erect a new sign in 2000 for the Millennium, the company donated £1000 towards the cost.

It replaced one of Harry Carter's traditional signs of the 1970s, which showed the mill on one side and a local fair on the other. The new sign, as well as depicting the mill on one of the arms with its missing sails restored, also shows a waggon heading for it, laden with corn, and on the third arm is St Nicholas's church. The animals' heads set into the sign - a pig, a sheep and a horse - represent the general rural flavour, the crown on top represents the Crown Inn just up the road, and the bright orange sun represents - eternal optimism?

The sign was erected on the original base, and the indecipherable plaque actually refers to Harry Carter's original well-worn sign, which as I write awaits a decision on its future.

GELDESTON

A wherry, wild duck, a fisherman – they're all here

An enthusiastic Norfolk lady wrote of this sign: 'If you love your Norfolk Broadland you will surely find in it all that appeals to you...' - and you can see what she means. The main feature is a splendid fully-rigged wherry, with wild duck flying in the distance and wild flowers in the foreground. In the spandrels are a fisherman, a yacht and a kingfisher.

But Geldeston is not actually by a Broad, it lies on the River Waveney, and that wherry is probably carrying corn to the local maltings. The river was used to transport goods and crops from the days of the Romans, who thoughtfully left behind a sacrificial vessel at Geldeston as a reminder of their presence. In more recent times beer was brought by boat to the isolated but very popular pub by Geldeston Lock. Most of the customers came that way too, but these days it can be more easily reached by car.

The sign was erected by the W.I. in 1972, during the Harry Carter sign-carving era, but this one was carved and painted by Mr C. Reeve of Mettingham. It was placed next to an equally well-preserved Coronation seat installed in 1937, and now there is a third 'date-marker', a boulder inscribed '2000'.

GIMINGHAM

Time moves on - and so has the sign

This is indeed a sign of the times, in more ways than one. It not only illustrates earlier times in the village, but its position demonstrates how changes are still taking place. Whenever a sub-post office closes it has an impact on the life of the village, but in Gimingham it also had an impact on the sign, which used to stand outside it. The post office became a private house and the sign had to find a new home. It now stands in quite a different location, outside the village hall.

Happily it survived the move, and so have most of the buildings which are shown on it. Only the watermill has gone - and of course the horse and tumbrel. But All Saints' church is still there, and perched on top of the sign is John of Gaunt's Hall, a well-preserved Jacobean house named after the Duke of Lancaster who held court at Aylsham, and features on that sign too. He held the manor of Gimingham from the King at a nominal rent of one mushroom - hence his coat of arms underneath.

Next to the Hall on the sign is the village pound, and this is still standing too. It is triangular, a design sometimes preferred by parishes, not for any aesthetic reason but because three walls are cheaper to build than four.

GOODERSTONE

The conversion of St George!

This must be one of the biggest village signs of its kind in Norfolk, and when I saw it, one of the brightest, because it was refurbished and re-gilded in 2000. There had also been some discreet adjustments to its design.

When it was erected by the parish council in 1996, the figure in armour was supposed to represent the Earl of Pembroke, a local knight who was killed in a tourney a few hours after his marriage in 1343. It resulted in his unfortunate bride being 'a maiden, a wife and a widow on the same day', as a leaflet in the parish church still observes. Unfortunately a local historian has since pointed out that this was impossible, because the Earl of Pembroke actually died in France in 1323.

The knight's shield was therefore skilfully adjusted to turn him into St George, who by a happy chance is patron saint of the parish church, already portrayed on the sign.

The large fish has also grown from a shoal of much smaller ones, and now accommodates the village's original name in the Domesday Book, Godestuna, and the words 'within the lands of Godric the Steward'. I wondered at first if the fish represented the 'tuna' in Godestuna, but it actually recalls a medieval trout fishery in the village. The River Gadder flows above it.

GREAT MASSINGHAM

A Premier takes the premier place

For many years the only village sign in Great Massingham was a well on the green with the name of the village above it in wrought iron. It is still there, but a rather grander sign now stands nearby, erected to mark the fiftieth anniversary of the end of the second World War.

It illustrates Great Massingham's history from medieval times to the present day, so a thirteenth-century monk tends his sheep opposite a modern farm-worker harrowing a field in his tractor. Above them flies, not only the Union flag, but the standard of the Royal Air Force, a reminder of the wartime airbase at Massingham.

In the background are the parish church and one of the five ponds in the village, which were probably fishponds for the monks of the Augustinian priory which used to stand by the green. There are vestiges of it at Abbey House.

The central figure is actually a non-resident, Sir Robert Walpole of Houghton Hall, who attended a private school in the village. The connection may seem a little tenuous, but it was enough to earn England's first Prime Minister a premier place on the sign.

GREAT MOULTON

A typical church and mill – but then there's the Rectory

This 1986 sign features the village's most distinctive buildings, clustered together in a somewhat tightly-knit group. Perhaps the most striking is the Old Rectory, an Italianate villa with a three-storeyed tower. Its entrance hall rises to a square lantern roof.

This rather exotic concoction was built for the Rev. J. S. Wigget in 1831, when country parsons could afford that sort of thing. According to Pevsner it was designed by W. J. Donthorn, who normally specialised in Tudor-Gothic, the style which most of the gentry preferred. This is thought to be his only classical building to survive unaltered, though needless to say it is no longer occupied by the Rector.

The old mill was burnt down in the early 1900s, and the railway arch is a reminder that the main line passes through the village. The apples are in memory of a local cider-maker, Will Bales. Finally there is St Michael's church, a rather more traditional building than the Old Rectory. It is mainly Norman with possibly Saxon origins. Some wall paintings were added in 1909, for which Pevsner, I am afraid, has only one word: 'hideous!'

GREAT RYBURGH

The maltings still malt, but the Gant has gone

The quaint old maltings on one side of the sign seem a far cry from the massive complex of buildings and silos which have replaced them today, and the equally quaint old horse-drawn waggon has given place to giant juggernauts, but at least the maltings still survive, and provide a lot of employment in the area. Indeed the business has expanded from its original site, and the old Crown Inn was bought up to be converted into its office.

Other traditional industries in the village have not fared so well. The buildings of a former foundry have been converted into small industrial units, and a granary has also closed down. The old watermill has gone too, but Mill House has been extended to make an attractively-sited nursing home.

Another traditional feature of Great Ryburgh, the May fair or Gant portrayed on the reverse side of the sign, disappeared much earlier, in 1902. The Gant was famous for its gooseberry pies, and when the sign was unveiled in 1976 to mark the golden jubilee of the Women's Institute, the W. I. President and another member baked two large gooseberry pies for the occasion.

GRESSENHALL

Underneath the spreading chestnut tree - a mini-plough

The sign has acquired an extra plaque since it was unveiled on the village green in 1978. Dated eleven years later, it records that Gressenhall won the John Haigh Shield for the best-kept village green. A dozen years later, one can still understand why. The Fairstead, as it is called, is fringed by magnificent chestnut trees, which offer convenient shade for outdoor tuition on a hot summer's day.

The trees on the sign, though, provide a backcloth for a splendid little metalwork plough, exact in every detail, which is attached to the front of it. The plough was made by George Bunning, whose family have been village blacksmiths for generations. Today George Bunning & Sons Ltd, Agricultural Engineers have rather more extensive business premises, but they are still just beside the green.

The sign is framed by a double arch, which symbolises the parish church, nearly a mile away. Gressenhall is probably best known these days for the expensively refurbished Rural Life Museum, but this is not featured. Perhaps a Victorian workhouse would not be the most attractive decoration for a prize-winning village green.

GRISTON

They may have grown a little older over the years

Harry Carter's 1973 portrayal of a gaily-garbed figure waving a sword at a personable young couple outside Griston Hall may not immediately call to your mind the legend of the Babes in the Wood; the babes do seem remarkably mature. But there can be no mistaking the emblems underneath of St Peter and St Paul, patron saints of the parish church.

According to the reliable *Folklore, Myths and Legends of Britain*, a small boy and girl were left in the care of an uncle by their dying father, Arthur Truelove, back in the sixteenth century. To gain their inheritance the uncle hired two ruffians to kill them in nearby Wayland Wood, but one of the ruffians took pity on them and killed his accomplice instead, then left the children to escape. Unfortunately they never found their way out of the wood and starved to death. It is said that a thoughtful robin covered their dead bodies with moss and leaves, and their small ghosts still wander in the wood. Hence the wail in 'Wailand'.

Actually the name covers a much larger area than the wood, and any cries that you hear are probably the blackheaded gulls that breed on Scoulton Mere (and feature on the Scoulton sign, on a later page). But it's still a good story.

HALVERGATE & TUNSTALL

Is half-a-gate better than none - or worse than half-a-heriot

When Halvergate teamed up with its tiny neighbour for a joint village sign, it was very convenient for Harry Carter, who carved it, that each of their churches was dedicated to the same pair of saints. St Peter and St Paul therefore share one side of the sign.

The gate between them could refer to 'Halver-gate', but the experts are not unanimous about the meaning of Halfriate, its original spelling in the Domesday Book (which is what the 1086 on the reverse of the sign refers to). It might mean half-a-gate - a curious conception - or it could derive from the Old English heregeatu, in which case it meant 'land for which half a heriot was paid'. Unless you know how much half a heriot was worth - which I don't - it is difficult to decide which is preferable.

The running hares, known as Halvergate Hares, are presumably connected with an old verse which also refers to Reedham Rats, Southwold Swine and Cantley Cats - a bizarre little menagerie. The drainage mill and heron on the reverse side are more understandable Broadland emblems. I gather there used to be an explanatory panel, which is always helpful, but now there is just the plaque which Halvergate won in the 1998 Best-kept Village competition.

HARDLEY &
LANGLEY

...or if you prefer, Langley and Hardley

This could be the only sign in Norfolk featuring a different village on each side. It was erected in 1988 by the local parish council, which happens to cover both Hardley and Langley - I will keep them in alphabetical order - and it was positioned so that, if you are going towards Hardley you see the Hardley side, and vice versa. Which is perfectly logical, but village signs are generally placed in the centre of the village, and this one can be a little confusing for visitors trying to work out which village they are actually in.

The Langley side - the one I happened to see first - shows Langley Abbey and one of its White Canons. Carol Carpenter, the local historian, tells me they were so called because they kept sheep (some are grazing beside this one) and their robes were made of sheepskin - with the tails still hanging from them. The wherry is bringing goods to Langley Staithe, which has a coal store on the quay. The plinth of the sign has stones from the ruined abbey.

Hardley is represented by the church and the Hardley Cross, which marked the boundary between the Norwich and Yarmouth river authorities and still stands near the junction of the Chet and the Yare. The geese are flying over Hardley Flood, the nearby nature reserve.

HEVINGHAM

Not a witches' coven, just where the brooms were made

When I first saw the brooms on the sign I rather hoped that Hevingham might have been a landing site for broomstick-borne witches, but alas, there is a more mundane explanation. Broom-making used to be a staple industry here, and it was one of the last of the broom-makers, a Mr Wymer, who suggested incorporating them in the sign. *Kelly's Directory* of 1888 records a local broom-maker called Samuel Medler, and appropriately it was Mr Walter Medler, chairman of the parish council, who unveiled these brooms some ninety years later.

The sign was carved by Harry Carter for the Women's Institute, and he positioned the brooms between two large trees, representing the many ancient oaks and chestnuts around the village. There are several near the church, and some of those in the churchyard are said to have been planted in the reign of James I. One is reputed to have a girth of nineteen feet.

The church itself can just be seen on the sign, in a rural setting which bears out Francis Blomefield's description of Hevingham in 1750, 'lying at the confluence of several tiny streams'.

HICKLING

'Behold the Seal' - and you can behold the Priory too

Hickling is probably best known these days for its Broad and its nature reserve, and there is a flavour of both on this 1974 sign, but pride of place is given to its former glory, the Augustinian priory founded by Theobald de Valoins in 1185. It was largely destroyed under Henry VIII, but Harry Carter carved one of his imaginative reconstructions of a building that has not actually been seen for over 450 years. The bits that survive are incorporated in the farm buildings at Priory Farm.

There were only ten Canons at the priory, but they owned property in over thirty parishes and King John granted them a charter for a weekly market. Hickling remained a market town until the 17th century.

A well-worn replica of the priory's ancient seal, inscribed in Latin 'Behold the Seal of St Mary of Hickling', is on the post below the sign, and there is a helpful plaque about the priory which completes this modest memorial to it. Sir William Wodehouse, who was granted the priory after the Dissolution, fared rather better. He has a handsome tomb in the church, which the monks helped to build.

The sign also shows a swallowtail butterfly and a bittern, which both breed around the Broad, plus one of the peat-diggers who created it, and a reed-cutter who trims the reed beds beside it.

HIGH KELLING

The sanatorium chapel that became a parish church

There was no such place as High Kelling a century ago, and it only became a civil parish in 1987. In Millennium year the High Kelling Society completed its evolution by providing this visible symbol of its independent existence.

The sign has the familiar emblems of a rural community - a squirrel, a rabbit and lots of trees - but its most significant feature is the unassuming little building in the centre. It links the origins of High Kelling and its present-day status, because originally it was the chapel of Bramblewood Sanatorium; now it is All Saints' parish church. The caduceus on the post below - two serpents entwined around a staff - is also a reminder of the village's medical origins.

It was the establishment of a TB sanatorium in what was then a sparsely-populated area which proved to be the foundation of a village community. Houses were built for the staff with some social facilities - a clubhouse, a chapel, a shop. The area became so well known for its healthy air that two more sanatoria were built, and although their functions changed after the war the community continued to grow, as more 'incomers' arrived. Eventually it achieved its own parish status, with its own parish council and parish church - and finally its own village sign.

HILGAY

A lifesaving rocket and a prizewinning band

For a visiting tourist this sign may be a little baffling. Only the bridge, which crosses the river at the entrance to the village, has an obvious significance. But why should a cannon be firing at the parish church? How can a three-masted sailing ship be battling through the waves in a village so far from the sea? And why the trumpet and the trombone?

There is a fascinating story behind the cannon, the church and the ship. Captain George William Manby, whose family owned the Wood Hall estate in Hilgay, invented the rocket-fired lifeline for saving lives at sea, and it is said he first tested his apparatus by firing a line over the church tower to an imaginary ship in distress. There was a rather entertaining re-enactment of his experiment in an Anglia TV series about Norfolk churches a few years ago.

The reason for the musical instruments is less dramatic but just as commendable. They represent Hilgay's prizewinning silver band, which had been going strong for about a century when the sign was erected in 1987, and it flourishes still. It has some twenty-five members, a youth section - and numerous trophies. In 2001 it was invited to play at Park House on the Sandringham royal estate.

HILLINGTON

Ancient walkers, steam trains, even dead whales - they all passed this way

The remarkable range of characters and features on the two sides of the sign cover just about every aspect of Hillington's history, from the walkers on the ancient Icknield Way to the trains that called at Hillington station until the line closed in 1963.

A wayside cross represents four such crosses which stood in the village; their remains are nearby. And the archer is Berner the Bowman (not to be confused with Bernie the Bolt, of postwar TV fame), who received from William the Conqueror the area then known as Hellingetun. There are the usual farm-workers and the parish church, plus a more unlikely feature for an inland village, a whale. When King's Lynn was a whaling port the whales were brought to this area to be processed, so that the smell should not offend the good burghers of Lynn.

The most impressive illustration on the sign, however, is the massive gateway to Hillington Hall, just across the road. It was originally the East Gate into Lynn, but in 1800 it was demolished and the Folkes family acquired it for their Hall. Present-day planning authorities might baulk at it, but in those days they were not the Folkes to argue mwith.

The sign was unveiled in 1996 by the Queen Mother, whose friend Lady Fermoy lived in the village.

HINGHAM

Off go the emigrants - and one of them was a Lincoln

In the 1630s some two hundred people from Hingham followed the earlier example of the Pilgrim Fathers and emigrated to America. They founded a settlement at Bare Cove on Massachusetts Bay, and it was given the name of their home town. This link between the two Hinghams has not been forgotten over the centuries, and there is another reminder of the mass emigration on the village sign. It was originally designed by Harry Carter in 1953 and replaced by an exact replica in 1989.

It shows a quayside with ships coming and going, and a token trio of emigrants waiting to leave - no doubt kept informed of the shipping movements by the chap with the telescope. Norwich Castle has been conveniently transported into the scene of departure, not to be exported to America but to symbolise one particular emigrant, a Hingham man who worked as a weaver in the city, presumably under the shadow of the castle. His name was Samuel Lincoln, direct ancestor of the sixteenth President of the United States.

It should be said that Swanton Morley also has a connection with him, as another branch of the Lincoln family lived there. But Hingham claims precedence, with a bust of Abe Lincoln in the church and a village hall which bears his name.

HOCKHAM MAGNA

Come blow your horns - or did you have to butt them?

This is Hockham's second village sign, in place of a wooden one carved by Harry Carter back in 1965, but both of them have commemorated a long-lost feature of village life, the Hockham Magna Horn Fair.

Explanations of the horn connection vary. The Hockham-born author Christopher Bush said his father told him about 'huge ox-horns with a hairy pad between', which strangers at the fair had to butt with their heads or pay a penalty. Another version has the horns being worn, Viking-style, by a villager appointed to chase and round up visitors, and this is the character portrayed on both the signs.

Harry Carter's horn-wearer was a giant-like figure, looming over the nervous-looking folk gazing up at him. His current successor looks far less menacing, and indeed he appears to be enjoying a swig out of a drinking horn, while the others seem to be largely ignoring him.

This is perhaps because the horn fair specialised in goods made of horn, from beakers to buttons. But whatever the significance of the name, the fair died out about 150 years ago, and the only visible reminders are two sets of horns in the village hall - and this sign.

HOCKWOLD-CUM-WILTON

The sign that disappeared - twice!

A few weeks after the sign was erected in 1974 it mysteriously disappeared. It had been taken as a joke by a locally-based American serviceman, but the villagers were not amused and nor were the local magistrates. They imposed a substantial fine.

Alarmingly, when I visited Hockwold a few months ago, the sign was missing again, but this time there turned out to be a very good reason - and it could hardly have been in a safer place. It was in Wayland Prison! Actually a number of local signs have been restored in the workshops there, and by now I hope the rejuvenated hounds on Hockwold's sign are back in position again, still chasing that hare. They are a reminder of Hockwold Coursing Club, which flourished between the wars.

Also on the sign is the Little Ouse, which marks the southern boundary of the village, and indeed the county. Hockwold and Wilton now form a civil parish and share the sign, so it shows St James's church, Wilton, with its fourteenth-century stone spire - a rare sight in Norfolk - as well as St Peter's, Hockwold, which is now redundant. The loaves underneath recall a local bread charity, the beehives were mentioned in the Domesday Book, and the chequerboard coat of arms is that of the Norman Lord of the Manor, the Earl de Warrenne.

HORSFORD

A Pyramid in the Alps? There's a good reason

Predictably, one side of the Horsford sign depicts a horse in a ford, but the picture on the reverse side, which is probably missed by motorists driving into the village, takes a little more explaining. It shows three young women apparently ascending to Heaven against a curiously mixed background of Pyramids, mountains, fir woods and a lake.

This is a replica of a window which was installed in the parish church in the 1890s in memory of three sisters, Edith, Dorothea and Nona Day. They all died of consumption within the space of eighteen months while they were still in their early twenties. They had gone abroad in the hope of finding different treatments. One died in Egypt, the other two in a sanatorium in Switzerland.

The smaller pictures in the spandrels represent former industries in the village: milling, brickmaking, weaving and flag-cutting, the flag in this case meaning peat. This was one of Harry Carter's more elaborate signs, made to mark the golden jubilee of the afternoon Women's Institute, and it is set in an attractive border of flowering shrubs. Unfortunately the road from Norwich is generally so busy these days that it is difficult to stop and appreciate it.

HUNSTANTON

The legendary St Edmund - and friend

The sign features St Edmund, who according to legend landed at Hunstanton from Germany in 855 AD to claim the throne of East Anglia. He had apparently intended to sail up the Waveney towards Thetford, East Anglia's principal centre, but a strong southerly wind blew his ship past the estuary, then conveniently changed direction at the right moment to blow him right round the east coast to Hunstanton - which faces west.

He is supposed to have landed under Hunstanton's famous striped cliffs at what became known as St Edmund's Point. Four centuries later a chapel was built on the cliff-top to commemorate his arrival. The ruins still survive, and so does the legend. Hunstanton's full name is Hunstanton St Edmund, he is patron saint of the parish church, and the town sign, erected in 1980, helps to perpetuate the story.

It may also illustrate another famous legend, because some say the dog beside him is Black Shuck, the sinister portent of death. But I prefer to think it is the wolf that is said to have guarded Edmund's severed head after his martyrdom by the Danes. When the king's followers came in search of his remains, the wolf obligingly cried 'Over here!'

Well, if you're going to have a legend on a town sign, let's make it a jolly good one...

INGOLDISTHORPE

Early W.I. Presidents? Not exactly...

The sign features two stately ladies, one in Quaker dress, the other in a long gown with a plumed hat, and as the emblem of the Women's Institute is just below them, an innocent stranger might assume there was some connection. Could they be a couple of early W.I. presidents, perhaps?

Certainly when the sign was designed and erected in 1968 the local W.I. selected them to represent the village rather than any males. They might have chosen Sir John Cremer, for instance, a seventeenth century local squire who became High Sheriff of Norfolk. As the W.I. themselves point out in their local history, this was a great honour for so small a village. But instead they honoured Agnes Biggs, a rector's daughter, and Mrs Eleanor Coates Tylden, a Lady of the Manor - not for any W.I. connection but because they were both local benefactresses.

In 1608 Agnes Biggs left £5 in her will for repairs to the church and £10 for the relief of the poor - substantial sums in those days. Mrs Tylden, who died in 1928 at the remarkable age of 105, also gave generously to the poor and provided the village hall. She was a friend of the Royal Family and on her 100th birthday, instead of the traditional letter from the Sovereign, Queen Mary came herself.

So, not exactly W.I. presidents - but I am sure they would have qualified.

ISLINGTON

'He loved the bailiff's daughter dear' - and here she is

Islington has seen a lot of changes. Lady Harrod's *Norfolk Guide*, which normally concentrates on church architecture rather than waxing sentimental, notes sadly: 'Here, in a wood where herons nested, was the 13th-century church, the Hall and some cottages. Now the trees are cut down, the church is partly roofless, the cottagers have moved to new houses nearer Tilney, and the park and woods have become a muddy expanse of potato fields.'

She must have seen it on a bad day. Even so, Islington has now lost its separate identity; all the road signs refer to Tilney cum Islington. Happily, however, its village sign survives, and it portrays two features of the old village which are still linked with Islington alone.

There are the herons, which moved to another wood nearby; it is now one of the largest heronries in the country. And the young lady lolling on the bank is the Bailiff's Daughter of Islington, immortalised in a famous ballad. The squire's son fell in love with her, they were parted and he thought she had died, but it all ended happily: 'She is here alive, she is not dead, and ready to be thy bride!'

I learned all this from Fred Ham, who was headmaster of the primary school. In 1978 he designed the sign and raised the funds for it, helped by the pupils and parents.

KING'S LYNN

Three signs: one gone, one retired, one still on duty

Between the 1950s and the 1970s three different signs were erected in King's Lynn - by three different organisations. Today only one of them is still functioning in its original role. It was made by Harry Carter in 1959 for the Business and Professional Women's Club, and after occupying one or two other sites during the past 40-odd years it can now be seen - if you can take your eyes off the traffic long enough - just off the Hardwick roundabout at the entrance to the town. A closer inspection will show that it has St Margaret on one side, the patron saint of the parish church, and on the other is Henry Bell, the architect who built the Custom House. Above them is the town's coat of arms.

A sign which used to stand on the Gayton Road, given by the Lynn branch of the National Council of Women, has now succumbed, and the third one, formerly near the Great Ouse and commissioned by the Borough Council, has returned 'home' and gone into retirement in the gardens of the Council offices in Chapel Street.

It shows a stylised version of the waterfront featuring all of Lynn's famous buildings in one group. St Margaret's church stands behind St George's Hall and the Guildhall, flanked on one side by the Red Mount Chapel, the Custom House and St Nicholas' chapel, and on the other by the Greyfriars Tower and the South Gate.

MARHAM

Take your pick – there's the old and the new

Several villages have replaced their original wooden signs with modern replicas in other materials, but Marham has done things slightly differently. In 1977 the local RAF station presented the original sign to mark the Silver Jubilee. It was carved by Harry Carter and erected outside the church. Then in Millennium year a metal one with a different design, painted by Brian McCabe, was put up at the entrance to the village - but the old wooden one still survived.

Since then the wood has deteriorated, and it is now planned to celebrate the Golden Jubilee by replacing it with an exact metal replica. So Marham will still have the distinction of displaying two village signs in two different styles on two different sites.

They do however contain similar features. They each have a ploughman, familiar symbol of farming, and a pre-war æroplane, recalling the earlier airfield which the RAF expanded during the war and again last year, when more Tornadoes returned home. Each sign features cherries, from the days when the village was known as Cherry Marham, and finally they each have a nun, recalling the Cistercian nunnery which stood opposite the church. She is Sister Barbara, the last Abbess, who confessed to an affair with the Prior of Pentney when the nunnery was dissolved by Henry VIII, and is still supposed to haunt the site.

MARTHAM

May I suggest you avoid the Viking, and look inside the church

The Viking on one side of the sign is obviously intent on a spot of rape and pillage - the lady and her friend seem to think so anyway. Certainly there were Vikings around in these parts, but to me the church of St Mary in the background is a little more intriguing, with its curious records of two local deaths.

First, the parish register records the burial in 1724 of Edward, 'base-born daughter of Mary Biggs'. This was not an early sex change but a mistake by a midwife, who got the baby's sex wrong. As the little girl was named Edward on the baptisms page, she had to be buried as 'Edward' a year later.

In the second case a memorial stone records Christopher Burroway's epitaph to Alice, 'in this life my sister, my mistress, my mother and my wife.' Here's how it happened. His father had an affair with his own daughter, producing baby Christopher, who was taken away and brought up elsewhere. When he returned as a young man he unknowingly worked for his mother-cum-sister, then married her - and only later discovered their complicated relationship. Not even the enterprising Harry Carter could design a sign to illustrate all that!

So when he carved this one in 1975 he just put a wherry and a wind pump on the reverse side. As far as I can see - and the sign is very worn - he also ignored the martens that gave the village its name. Perhaps they led complicated lives too.

MILEHAM

Are the last of the FitzAlans in Utah USA?

A lot more is now known about Mileham Castle and its owners than in 1973, when Harry Carter featured it on the village sign. Twenty-five years later archaeologists literally unearthed more information from the castle ruins. They established that the castle motte or mound was thirty feet high, surrounded by a moat and surmounted by a keep, though there is little to see of it now. Nevertheless Harry Carter managed to picture the keep, with a solitary Norman soldier gallantly defending it. On the post he put a replica of an ancient sword found in the village, and the post itself was set in a base made of flints from the parish coalhouse which used to be on the site.

However there has been a more recent addition to the post. In 1983 an American gentleman from Utah called Wallace Houston came to Mileham to check through the parish records. He established - to his own satisfaction at least - that he was descended from the Norman FitzAlan family who built the castle and owned it for nearly four centuries.

He thereupon 'gifted' to the parish council the metal plaque that is now displayed on the post below the sword. It lists the FitzAlans and their family crests, and also bears the crest of William the Conqueror, but it is not clear if he was related to Mr Houston too.

NORTH CREAKE

Not just a pretty arch...

The arch which frames the sign is not just there for decoration. It is a reminder of Creake Abbey, which now lies in ruins in a peaceful corner north of the village. Sir Robert de Nerford built it for the Augustinians in the early thirteenth century, and pilgrims dropped in on the way to the shrine at Walsingham. The monks at Creake Priory, as it then was, may have envied their colleagues at Walsingham for attracting all the trade, but perhaps they felt better when they were granted the status of an abbey by Henry III, while the much larger priory at Walsingham was ignored.

Fortune swung the other way again when part of Creake Abbey was destroyed by fire in 1484, and it was dissolved in 1506 after a disastrous outbreak of plague. Then along came Henry VIII and the Dissolution of the Monasteries - and honours were even...

The sign was erected in 1998 to a design chosen by the villagers. It shows a blacksmith working at his anvil, but the Old Forge is now the Post Office, and of course the ploughman's horses have long since gone. St Mary's church survives, and it contains a permanent reminder of the old abbey up the road. A stone from the ruins is incorporated in the altar.

NORTH ELMHAM

A stone Saxon Cathedral? Well, perhaps not

There are tourist signs around North Elmham pointing to 'The Saxon Cathedral', and for many years - including the 1950s when I lived in the village - it was thought that the ruins behind the former George & Dragon Inn were indeed those of a stone cathedral built in Saxon times. So when the village got Harry Carter to re-create a stone building on the sign to celebrate the 1300th anniversary of the founding of the See in AD 673, they inscribed the plaque:

'It depicts the first stone cathedral (c. 1000) which replaced the original timber building.'

But time moves on. Pubs disappear - the George & Dragon is now a private house - different experts produce different findings. Today the information boards at the ruins state firmly that the original timber cathedral 'remained in use as a parish church until about 1100'. Then the Norman Bishop de Losinga erected a replacement church nearby, the timber building was demolished, and a stone chapel was built on the site for his personal use. It is the remains of this chapel which survive today; there never was a 'stone cathedral'.

Never mind, it's a jolly nice sign. But I think the bishop standing under his 'cathedral' is looking a bit bewildered.

NORTH REPPS

Siting, content, presentation - they all get maximum points

This meets all my criteria for an ideal village sign. It is easy to find in a prominent position; it features a positive cornucopia of intriguing objects with local connections, from a breeches buoy to the radiator of a Rolls Royce; and rarest of all, there is an inscription giving a comprehensive explanation - very necessary in some cases - of what they all mean.

Here's just a flavour. One shield represents St Benet's Abbey, because the last Abbot was William Ruggs or Repps, who was born here. The lute-like instrument is a cittern, recalling another local man, John Playford, who wrote *A Booke of Newe Lessons for the Cittern and Gittern* in 1652. The set of fetters is a reminder that Sir Thomas Fowell Buxton, a noted nineteenth-century anti-slavery campaigner, lived at North Repps Hall.

The plough does not just represent farming. This Gallas Plough was developed in North Repps Foundry in 1830 and was in use until the 1920s. As for the breeches buoy and the Rolls Royce radiator, the buoy was tested at North Repps Hall and Henry Royce convalesced here for six months while developing the Silver Ghost.

Then we have the smuggler's barrel and the Revenue officer's post, the railway bridge, the poppies, the other shield - all explained on the post. Indeed a sign of great thoroughness!

NORTH RUNCTON

Gurney's Hall has gone - but Bell's church survives

The coat of arms on the post belongs to the Gurney family of Runcton Hall, which was built for Daniel Gurney, youngest brother of Elizabeth Fry, in 1834. He and his descendants were local landowners or parsons - or both - for generations. The Hall was demolished in 1965, much to the regret of experts such as Sir Nikolaus Pevsner, who recalled in particular its elegant staircase, acquired from a house in King's Lynn. 'What happened to it after the house was demolished?' he asked. I hope it's back in King's Lynn.

The prominent figure on the sign is not Daniel Gurney but another local resident with an interest in architecture. Henry Bell was the eighteenth century architect who designed the famous Custom House in King's Lynn. He was twice Mayor of the borough, but he actually lived in North Runcton and he designed the parish church, which is featured behind him on the sign. He also donated £15 towards its cost - and presumably waived his usual fee.

All Saints' took ten years to build, and was completed in 1713. There have been some adjustments since, but it is still considered one of the finest buildings of its period in Norfolk, and it shows up well on the sign.

PASTON

A sign of earlier times: could this be the oldest swinger?

I have yet to find another sign that hangs instead of stands, as well as being nearly fifty years old, so this could be the oldest swinger of its kind in the county. It was erected to mark the Queen's Coronation, and it rather reminds me of the signs that hang proudly outside venerable tailoring establishments, showing they hold the Royal Warrant.

It features, however, not a bespoke hacking jacket or a pair of plus fours, but reminders of the Paston family - their famous Letters, and their equally famous Great Barn. A scroll and quill pen represent the correspondence which passed between Margaret Paston and her husband during the turbulent fifteenth century, when John Paston was often away from home and his wife was left on her own to defend - sometimes quite literally - the family estates.

The magnificent barn built by their sixteenth-century descendant William Paston is one of the showpieces of rural Norfolk and has its place on the sign, alongside the nineteenth-century Stow Mill, which dominates the coast road to Mundesley. Both have been restored, and when I was last in Paston the sign was being restored too, but it should now be back in place - and still swinging.

SAHAM TONEY

Roger's put his hat on - and the monks have had a good day

The village acquired its unusual name when Roger de Toeni, a grandson of William the Conqueror's standard-bearer - and such connections were useful - became Lord of the Manor. He added his Norman family name to Saham, which came from a Saxon word meaning 'homestead by the lake'. When Harry Carter carved a sign in 1953 he ingeniously combined the two ingredients of the name, and put Roger de Toeni beside the lake. He had a chubby white dog with him, and there were two monks fishing on the lake in a boat, recalling the days when monks from the Cluniac priory at Castle Acre were granted permission to come and replenish their stocks twice a year.

When that sign was replaced the new one retained the same theme, but Roger de Toeni now protects his bald head, previously uncovered, with a floppy hat, and his dog looks a lot slimmer and sprightlier. The two monks are looking more cheerful too; maybe they have increased their catch since Harry Carter's day.

However, the post still bears a shield with an M-shaped emblem, which looks rather like the Motorola trademark - but this does not mean they have sponsored the sign. It is actually a heraldic symbol from the arms of the Hastings family.

SALHOUSE

Very different from Salthouse – it's down to a 't'

The name of the village only differs from Salthouse by one letter, which can confuse the tourists - and the postmen - but the origins of these names are totally different. They reflect their different locations. Salthouse derives rather obviously from a house where salt was stored, and is of course by the sea. Salhouse, on the other hand, is named after sallows, small willows, which grow here in profusion

Harry Carter was not one to slip up over this sort of thing, and there is no trace of a salt-house on the Salhouse sign which he carved. Instead he created a framework of two willow trees, bending towards each other to form an archway with their branches.

Beneath it are two men working among the reeds, which are also prolific here; Salhouse has always been a centre for the reeding and thatching industries. Between them on Salhouse Broad is another traditional feature of Broadland, a Norfolk wherry. Underneath is the insignia of the Women's Institute, which erected the sign in 1973.

SCOULTON

How does 'kyauu kyauu kyau' sound to you?

It is not often that a gull takes pride of place on a village sign, but these gulls are rather special. They are the famous Scoulton black-headed gulls, known sometimes as laughing gulls because of their curious breeding call. They could also be called crying gulls, because their plaintive cries over Wayland Wood used to be attributed to the wandering spirits of the unfortunate Babes in the Wood (see Griston sign). The cry is described in a bird manual as 'kyauu kyauu kyau' - note the subtle change in the final note! Try it and see if you laugh or cry...

There is another special feature of these birds. Like most other gulls they are normally found near the sea, and the same manual confirms that they are found by fresh water 'only on passage'. But the Scoulton gulls seem to spend a remarkable length of time on the island in Scoulton Mere; they even breed there. Certainly they provide a great attraction for ornithologists.

The sign was erected in 1983. It also features Captain John Wayland of Woodrising Hall, who was said to have sold the gulls' eggs to his upmarket acquaintances in the guise of far more expensive plovers' eggs. The parish church, which stands well outside the village, is appropriately placed in the far distance.

SHERINGHAM

'Adorned by both sea and pines' - and the odd lobster

The dark unpainted sign is not too easy to spot against the modern brick façade of Sheringham Post Office, but it is worth taking a closer look to see the detail. It was erected in the era of Harry Carter's brightly painted signs, so this plain Iroco wood carving by Joe Dawes of Saxthorpe must have provided quite a striking contrast.

The two pine cones on the shield represent the pinewoods that lie behind the town, and the ship of course indicates the proximity of the sea. I gather the helmet is just an heraldic decoration, rather than an emblem of some medieval Sheringham knight, but the lobster on top of it is more significant. It is a reminder of the fishing industry which used to thrive at Sheringham, and still continues today to a lesser degree. Lobsters are not quite so common now as their humbler relation, the Cromer (or Sheringham) crab.

The inscription under the coat of arms is not one I have come across before. I am told it means 'Adorned by both sea and pines'. Mr Bob Lord, who designed the sign, was by profession an architectural designer, but he obviously knew his Latin too.

SLOLEY

Don't think 'slowly' - think 'sloes'

The name of this village has always epitomised for me the gentle pace of life in rural Norfolk - so I confess I was disappointed to learn from the sign that Sloley has nothing to do with lack of velocity. In the Domesday Book it was spelt Slaleia, from the Old English words meaning blackthorn - yes, sloes - and 'leah' meaning a grove. I shall never feel quite the same about Sloley again...

Nevertheless this is a very handsome cast-iron sign, with those disillusioning sloe bushes on one side of St Bartholomew's church and a wheatsheaf on the other, to provide an agricultural flavour. The three saxes or flaying-knives on the shield below recall the martyrdom of St Bartholomew, who is said to have been flayed alive. By contrast the cheerful character in the foreground, nonchalantly dangling one leg over the front of the sign and grasping a large goblet, requires more explanation. I found it in the official description of the sign at the time it was unveiled in 1995:

'It may be taken as a capricious evocation of Ralph de Beaufour, brother of the Bishop of Thetford and Sloley's great Norman landowner, seen fortifying himself with a goblet of eau de vie.' He was obviously a chap who liked to take life - well, slowly!

SOUTHERY

A wherry and a windmill, fine - but a lighthouse?

At first glance this sign looks straightforward enough. Southery has the Great Ouse flowing past to the west, and the Little Ouse and the Wissey are not far away, so it is understandable that there is a wherry on a river in the foreground. A windmill is also a traditional feature of this area, and the cottage on the right looks equally appropriate. But on the left, on top of a hill - which is unusual enough in itself around here - can that be a lighthouse?

Admittedly parts of the Fens are below sea level, and this part in particular was regularly flooded until a new channel was cut and the Great Ouse was widened. But the sea is actually some twenty miles away. Incorporating a lighthouse in the village sign might seem a little pessimistic.

Only a local can tell you why it is there. Until a few years ago there was a tall house in the village at the end of Avenue Row. There was a recess in the gable-end, and in the recess there used to be a lantern. Inevitably the house became known as the Lighthouse, and when the sign was erected in 1977 I suppose it seemed appropriate to include a symbolic image of this local landmark. Now the Lighthouse has been demolished, but the one on the sign lives on, to baffle visitors and later generations.

SPORLE

A sign of the changing times

This modern sign is the elaborate successor to a traditional wooden one carved by Harry Carter for the Women's Institute in 1972. His version depicted the Benedictine priory in Sporle which was dissolved in the fifteenth century. The wooden sign did not exactly dissolve, but in 1984 it was considered too dilapidated to be restored, and this new sign was designed by Mr Kenneth Denton, who happens to live in Priory Farm, just across the road.

It shows some architectural details from the priory and portrays St Mary, patron saint of the priory and the church, and St Catherine, whose martyrdom on a wheel is depicted in the church. The heraldry represents Matthew Halworthy, a local benefactor whose trust still helps the children of the village, and Edward Nelson, a former Rector who is interred in the church with his two daughters.

I can take no credit for being able to explain these less-than-obvious features of a rather complex design. Happily all the information is set out on a plaque beneath the sign.

SPROWSTON

It's not a falcon, just a rather superior crow

This is not the easiest sign to spot from a passing car. It stands at the corner of a large junction on the busy Wroxham road, and even if you dare to take your eyes off the traffic the black metalwork is inclined to merge into the dark foliage behind it. But it is worth taking a closer look, because this sign is unique. It was made by the pupils of Sprowston secondary school, under the guidance of their metalwork teacher, Mr Piggin. He could be Sprowston's equivalent to Swaffham's Harry Carter, once woodwork master at Hamonds Grammar School, who with his pupils made many of Norfolk's carved wooden signs, but so far as I know this was the only sign produced by Mr Piggins' class.

It shows the old postmill often painted by John Crome, which was burnt down in 1933. Above the parish church there flies a bird which might be a falcon, because there is a Falcon Road in Sprowston and one of the local Women's Institutes has the same name. I am assured, however, by a member of the older-established Sprowston W.I., which was involved in providing the sign, that the bird is a crow, or corbie. It is a pun on Corbet, a leading local family in the seventeenth and eighteenth century who adopted it as their emblem. The sign's oak post dates back nearly as far; it came from a 200-year-old barn in Colney.

SUTTON

Two kinds of sails – but the wherry has long since gone

The sign features Sutton's two main claims to fame, one past, one very much present; indeed you can hardly miss it. Sutton Mill is the largest in Norfolk, a nine-storey tower mill which measures eighty feet to the top of its cap. It was first erected in 1789 but had to be rebuilt some seventy years later after a disastrous fire. The last corn was ground in 1940, and it stood derelict for many years, but it was restored in the 1970s and continues to dominate the landscape.

The mill house is quite grand too. As Sir Nikolaus Pevsner observed in his *Buildings of England*, 'Business must have been good...'

The wherry represents another business which once prospered at Sutton, but it is a long time since wherries not only sailed here but were built here. This was one of the Broadland villages where navigable cuts were dug out in the eighteenth and nineteenth centuries to link them with the main waterways. In this case it linked Sutton with the River Ant.

The original sign was carved by Harry Carter for the Women's Institute in 1977. Since then it has had to be replaced by a copy, but it still stands on the same base, and retains the distinction of being one of the few signs in Norfolk with its own custom-built seat.

TAVERHAM

St Walstan scythed here – and found God among the furrows

St Walstan has the distinction of featuring on two Norfolk signs, at the beginning and the end of his final journey. The one at Bawburgh, where he was born and buried, is featured in the first *On the Verge*. The second, at Taverham, recalls how this son of a wealthy Saxon couple came to the village to toil in the fields, giving away his possessions, looking after the sick and needy, and as one writer put it, 'finding God among the furrows'. Legend has it that before he died he asked that his body be put in a cart drawn by two white oxen. They should set off on their own, and wherever they stopped, he should be buried. In Taverham's present-day traffic this would have been distinctly hazardous, but the oxen made their way safely out of the village and by a happy chance – or divine guidance? – took Walstan back to Bawburgh, where his shrine became a noted place of pilgrimage.

The Taverham sign shows his haloed figure standing in a field by the tree-lined River Wensum. He holds a cross and a scythe, ready for any eventuality – be it spiritual or agricultural. And those trees are not just for decoration; they represent an avenue of beeches planted in Taverham to celebrate the victory at Waterloo.

TERRINGTON ST CLEMENT

Sheep and strawberries, yes – but what about the shield?

When the W.I. asked Harry Carter to design a sign in 1977 to mark the silver jubilee, he had a wealth of subjects to choose from. The most obvious was the famous 'Cathedral of the Marshes', the largest village church in Marshland. Then there was the reclamation of the marshes by the Romans and others, and even the salt-making industry in the Middle Ages, in the area still known as the Saltings. All good Harry Carter material.

However, he liked to delve into the less familiar pages of local history too, and although he has put sheep and strawberries into the spandrels, both prolific in this area over the years, the sign itself is devoted to an obscure coat of arms and a Latin motto, which must baffle visitors – and perhaps some of the locals too.

The arms are not those of the Lovells of Lovell Hall, who come to mind first, nor of the Bentincks, one of whom made the village safe after the 1607 floods by building bigger embankments. They are the arms of Sir Andrew Snape Hamond, a local landowner whose son became Admiral of the Fleet in 1862 – in which role he might have ensured a speedy rescue for the villagers if those embankments collapsed. Hence I suppose the motto 'Prepared and Faithful'.

THORNAGE

From falconry to foundrywork – and a Bishop at the Hall

In the fifteenth century Bishop James Goldwell not only left his mark on Norwich Cathedral – his 'gold-well' rebus can still be seen on the presbytery roof bosses – but also on his manor-house at Thornage Hall where he had a deer park. The Hall and the Bishop are shown on one side of the village sign, which was unveiled in 1977 by Lord Hastings, a descendant of the Astleys who later owned the Hall.

The reverse side shows a scene in the local foundry, once well-known for its brass and ironwork. The foundry has long since closed and is now a private house, but several of its products survive in the village and the county.

The bird at the top of the sign represents an earlier local activity that was no doubt just as well-known in its time. Apparently Bishop Goldwell and his men were very fond of falconry, just the kind of obscure historical connection that Harry Carter liked to illustrate on his signs. This is still his original carving, but it has had at least two restorations. The first was carried out some time ago in the workshops of Wayland Prison, and the latest was last year.

THORPE ABBOTTS

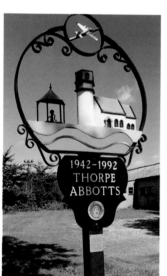

A wartime link is commemorated – with a bit of a 't'ser

This is more than just a village sign, it is a tribute to Anglo-American relations in general and the local link with one American Air Force unit in particular. It was unveiled in 1992 by the colourfully-named Owen 'Cowboy' Rowane, president of the 100th Bomb Group Association USA, to commemorate the Group's arrival at Thorpe Abbotts airfield, Station 139, in June 1942. The sign was given jointly by the villagers and members of the Association in the States.

The plaque on which all this information is so helpfully given was provided by two past chairmen of the Association. Their spelling of the village's name, the same as on the sign, is interesting. Some reference books refer to Thorpe Abbots with one 't', others seem undecided. Lady Harrod's *Norfolk Guide*, for instance, gives it double 't', then goes on to refer to the local mansion as Thorpe Abbots Place.

Lady Harrod's *Norfolk Guide*, for instance, gives it double 't', then goes on to refer to the local mansion as Thorpe Abbots Place.

The mansion was demolished in 1963 and does not appear on the sign. Instead it shows Thorpe Abbots church (as Pevsner spells it, though the Diocesan Directory prefers Abbotts), and the village pump, complete with its little roof. To complete the design an American 'Flying Fortress' flies overhead. I hope they returned safely, perhaps in time for 't' – or did they prefer a double?

THORPE END

The Unfortunate Case of the Disappearing Gardeners

This sign has experienced some dramatic changes since it was erected in 1965 to mark the golden jubilee of the W.I. movement. It started off as a simple oak tree, carved in dark oak and covered by a triangular 'roof'. The village's name and the relevant dates were beneath. Then when the movement's diamond jubilee came along, followed by the Queen's silver jubilee in 1977, the W.I. decided to celebrate both by up-dating the sign.

A wrought-iron frame was added, 'Garden Village' was inserted underneath, again with the relevant dates, and a gardening couple were placed on each side of the tree. It thus became one of the few village signs featuring characters in modern dress.

Another plaque was added in 1979 for being judged best-kept village, but apart from that the gardeners remained undisturbed until the autumn of 2001. I visited Thorpe End, armed with John Bacon's photograph – and found they had disappeared. I assumed that, like many other signs during the Millennium years, the figures had been removed for re-painting, but alas, vandals had broken them off and taken them away.

Fortunately they were retrieved a few days later, albeit badly damaged. The parish council had them re-welded and re-enamelled, and by now they should be back on the sign and busy with their gardening again.

TROWSE

He's not exactly Tarzan, so why is he up that tree?

Unless you are a student of Old English or Old Norse you may well be baffled by that bleary-eyed character peering out of a window in a tree. Certainly the two passers-by seem somewhat startled. It is one of Harry Carter's more challenging signs.

According to the experts, the name Trowse derives from 'treo' in Old English or 'tre' in Old Norse, and 'hus', which in both languages meant 'house'. But why name a village after a tree-house?

It is assumed that the area used to be flooded regularly by the River Yare, and villagers had to build their houses on stilts – or even took to the trees! On the other hand, perhaps children enjoyed playing in tree-houses just as much as today, and the idea caught on with the grown-ups. Either way, it was chance that Harry Carter could not miss.

Underneath are the emblems of the W.I., who erected the sign to mark their golden jubilee, and the Colman family, who were local benefactors as well as the major local employer at their nearby factory. They lived at Crown Point Hall, which later became Whitlingham Hospital.

WELLS-NEXT-THE-SEA

Distinctly nautical – except perhaps for that plough?

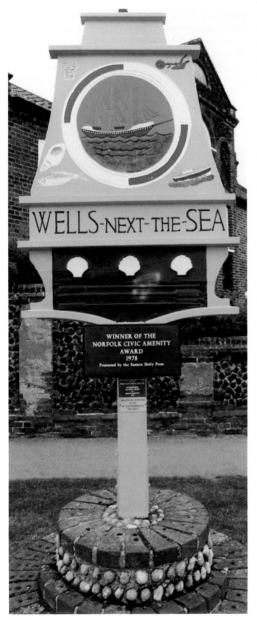

When the Regatta and Carnival Committee provided a town sign to mark the Queen's silver jubilee, it decided, very understandably, to devote its theme almost entirely to maritime matters. It recalls the town's historical role as a busy seaport, as well as the continuing activities of the fishermen and the Wells lifeboat. Even the sheaf of corn in one corner can be linked with the export of grain from the granary on the quay, rather than the farms that produced it.

The sign's central feature is a sailing ship to represent those earlier days. A lifebuoy surrounds it, and there is a lifeboat below. The old lifeboat house near the quay, now housing the harbourmaster's office and a maritime museum, goes back to the days when the boat had to be rowed or hauled by horses down the mile-long channel to the sea. Nearby is a memorial to eleven lifeboatmen who were trapped and drowned in 1880 when the boat overturned and its mast became embedded in the sand.

In another corner of the sign are a fish and a whelk, and below there are more shellfish and some oars. Only the plough in the remaining corner has no connection with the sea - or can it be a symbol of the days when mariners steered by the stars?

WIGGENHALL ST GERMANS

So don't hang another gamebird on the old oak tree

If you want to see this sign, make sure you come into St Germans from the King's Lynn direction, because it is not in the usual central position but out on the Lynn road. And even if you drive out of St Germans on that road you may still miss it because the reverse side is blank. Once you have managed to find it you may still not understand it, unless you are familiar with the legend of St Germanus.

It is one of those stories that is so unlikely that it deserves to be true. Germanus, Duke of Burgundy, was a great hunter who followed the tradition of hanging his trophies on a tree – hence the dead birds. The local Bishop disapproved and had the tree felled, which annoyed Germanus more than somewhat. But then the Bishop had a dream that he was about to die and that Germanus – rather surprisingly – was his chosen successor. He forthwith ordained the startled Duke, who then became devoted to his new calling and did indeed become a bishop – hence the mitre.

He came to England in 429 AD, and presumably a connection was established with this obscure corner of the Fens. Hence the dedication of the church, the name of the village, a set of bench-ends in the church depicting the legend – and this sign.

WIMBOTSHAM

It's all right – it's one of ours!

An RAF bomber is flying over Wimbotsham church again after an extensive refurbishment of the village sign last year. The plane is a reminder of the wartime airbase which was sited nearby, but in fact the village's aeronautical connections go back much further than the last war. It is recorded in a local directory that a balloonist landed here one early morning in 1835, having flown up from London overnight. It

must have caused quite a sensation locally in those early days of manned flight, but it seems that one down-to-earth farmer took it calmly enough to invite the intrepid fellow to join him for breakfast before resuming his flight to North Runcton.

St Mary's church, of course, goes back still further. It has two splendid doorways and a chancel arch dating back to the Normans, and the tower shown on the sign is fifteenth century. The original designer of the sign in the 1970s was Mrs Doris Bowgen, who used different-coloured woods to make the plane and the church stand out against a darker panel. It was erected in 1979 after local societies had collected funds to mark the Queen's silver jubilee two years earlier.

WOOD NORTON

Not just a pretty sign – it has a seat too

After overcoming various local difficulties Wood Norton rounded off its Millennium projects in June, 2001, with the unveiling of this sign on the little triangular green in the heart of the village. It was previously occupied by a water hydrant and a postbox – which I gather were part of the difficulties.

The old village school across the road is now privately occupied, and the local children go to school by a bus which stops near the sign. With these and other passengers in mind, an attractive wooden seat has been provided around its base – a fairly rare combination, though Sutton thought of it as far back as 1977.

The double-sided sign features the brick-towered parish church of All Saints' with an impressive array of gravestones in the foreground. One of the shields represents Christ's College, Oxford, which was given the Lordship of Wood Norton by Henry VIII. The sombre black shield represents the Norris family, who were local squires for generations. A member of the family, the Revd Malcolm France, who spent his childhood in the village, was present at the unveiling ceremony with his wife and children.

WORSTEAD

A sign tied together by wool

All three features on the sign – the sheep, the church, the coat of arms – are linked with the industry that brought fame and fortune to the village in the fourteenth century, and helped it prosper for five hundred years. Thousands of sheep in the area provided the wool for Worstead's world-famous cloth, which in turn provided the money for building the massive St Mary's church. The shield bears the arms of the local de Worstede family; like worsted cloth they adapted their name from Worstead, though slightly differently.

Many of the weavers were Flemish, encouraged to come to England by Edward III and his Flemish-born wife. They were attracted to this part of Norfolk because the countryside was similar to their own – and more importantly, Norfolk sheep provided the right kind of wool.

In its heyday Worstead had two churches, but St Andrew's has been replaced by the houses in St Andrew's Close. However, some of the weavers' houses still survive, and in the 1970s a Guild of Weavers was re-formed. The looms were first installed in St Mary's church, and are now in the Baptist church at Meeting Hill. An annual crafts festival has been revived, helping to recall Worstead's past glory, and of course there is Harry Carter's sign –though when I saw it last it was in need of a little reviving as well.

WORTHING

Why did the Roman lose his helmet? And how did it get in the river?

This is one of the latest signs erected to mark the new Millennium. Worthing is a tiny community of some seventy people, and they had never had a village sign before, so it was a notable achievement, even if it did not reach completion until the summer of 2001.

Most of the money for it was raised by the villagers, and one of them, Ian Lothian, actually carved it. The design was by Gordon Cooper of Dereham and follows a familiar theme – the little round-towered parish church, the old mill and the River Wensum, which flows past the village. The most distinctive feature, however, is the handsome Roman helmet on top of the sign, a replica of one that was found in the river in the 1960s.

It posed an interesting riddle, because nobody is quite sure how it got there, or what happened to its owner. But archaeologists say there was a Roman farmstead near the site of the present church, which was later taken over by the Saxons. Worthing's name comes from the Old English for a yard around a homestead, so perhaps the Saxon farmer found the helmet lying about in his yard and chucked it in the river. If any descendants of the original Roman settler want to reclaim the family heirloom, it is now in Norwich Castle Museum.

WRAMPLINGHAM

A village sign that made a real splash

Wramplingham may be a very small village, with little more than the parish church and the former millpond still surviving from much earlier days, but it does have a very ingeniously-sited sign. They had the choice, I suppose, to put it by the church or by the pond, but they decided to make a real splash and put it in the pond itself. It was installed in 1980, and it must have been built on firm foundations because it stands there still.

The design recalls the original use of the pond and shows the mill that used to stand beside it, with its impressive water-wheel. Next to the mill on the sign is a tree, which I gather was made of copper, so that in due course it would become appropriately green. To some degree it has worked, but unfortunately the other natural effects of ageing and weather have played their part too, and some of the metalwork is showing signs of wear. As it turns out the positioning of the sign may have been a mixed blessing. It certainly protected it from possible vandalism, but it must be very awkward to carry out regular maintenance work. Fortunately – and this is another plus for the choice of the site – it can only be viewed at a distance, so any defects are difficult to spot. All things considered, a memorable sign to end this book.